CW00350395

HOW
TO
MAKE
GREAT
DECISIONS

HOW TO MAKE GREAT DECISIONS

FR. MIKE SCHMITZ

WELLSPRING

North Palm Beach, Florida

wellspring

Design by Ashley Wirfel

ISBN: 978-1-63582-066-9 (hardcover)
ISBN: 978-1-63582-080-5 (ebook)

10   9   8   7   6   5   4   3   2   1

Printed in the United States of America

FIRST EDITION

TABLE OF CONTENTS

. . . .

ONE:
THE CURE FOR EXPRESSIVE INDIVIDUALISM
1

TWO:
THREE LEVELS OF VOCATION
9

THREE:
DECISIONS AND DISCERNMENT
23

FOUR:
THREE QUESTIONS
33

FIVE:
THE DOOR
41

SIX:
QUESTONS AND ANSWERS
49

ONE:
THE CURE FOR EXPRESSIVE INDIVIDUALISM

WHEN IT COMES to any type of discernment, it's really important to understand what is it that we're discerning. For instance, we could look at our lives and say, "Okay, I want to have this" or "I want to have that." Whether it's my career, my relationships, or my finances, we tend to approach everything centered around ourselves. We say, "I'm going to discern what God wants for my life."

Now, that word *my* is a really interesting word. It implies some sense of ownership. But in a deeper Christian sense, even my life is not really mine. St. Paul says this: "You are not your own; you were bought with a price" (1 Corinthians 6:19–20). Even before you are a Christian, you have to say that your life is not, strictly speaking, *your* life in the same way, for instance, that some material object is yours. C. S. Lewis used the example of a teddy bear. In *The Screwtape Letters* he says when we talk about our teddy bear,

3

we refer to something we could tear apart if we wanted to—because it belongs to us; it's *ours*. And that's how we refer to our lives—our home, our mom, our God, our life. We talk about our life or our God in the same way we talk about inanimate objects. "It's my life," we say. Therefore, we could do whatever we wanted with it. We could make a shipwreck of it if we chose to.

Or we think the goal of our life is to maximize our happiness—to find self-fulfillment or self-expression. In fact, a lot of times when we say we're discerning what to do with our life, we're really trying to figure out what will make us the happiest. What kind of relationship will make me the happiest? What kind of career will make me happiest? And when we approach it like that, we find ourselves in a bind, because all of a sudden, it's no longer about anyone other than me; it's all about me.

If we approach discernment with self-expression or self-fulfillment as our goal, we're looking at it the wrong way, and not only because it isn't "my life." Stop and think of all the options you have in your life right now. Barry Schwartz, a sociologist, did a study on what he called "the paradox of choice." He starts by saying, "Having choices is really, really good." It's great to have a lot of options out there, right? You go to the grocery store, and you don't just have spaghetti sauce. You have eighty-three different kinds of spaghetti sauce. You don't just have some salad dressing; you have 132 kinds of salad dressing for every possible taste you could possibly want.

Or what about going to the store to buy a pair of jeans? Those of you who have been living for a while know that back in the day, if you went shopping for jeans, you would go to the store, and they would have brands like Wrangler and Levis, or maybe even Jordache. Basically you'd have a few options that worked with your waist size and your inseam, you'd pick the one that fit the best, and you'd be on your way. But today there are boot cut jeans, skinny jeans, super-skinny jeans, baggy jeans, super-baggy jeans—there are so many choices, and they have to fit perfectly, or they're not the right jeans.

In other words, being good enough is no longer good enough. How many of us look at our lives like this when it comes to any decision we have to make? I have to point out, though, if something is good enough, that means it *actually is good enough*. But in our minds, "good enough" has come to mean "not good enough." Why? Because we're after "the *perfect*"—that thing that will make us maximally happy, that will maximize our self-expression, that thing that will give us the most joy, the most contentment, the most fulfillment, the most expression. Good enough is no longer good enough. And in that kind of world, the perfect becomes the enemy of the good.

I hear people say all the time, "Oh I'm discerning. . . ." One of my fellow priests once said, "Ever since discernment became popular, no one has made a decision." Everyone is too busy discerning. What do you really mean when you say, "I'm discerning my vocation," or, "I'm discerning what God wants"? You really mean, "I'm just thinking about it."

True discernment is more than just *thinking* about something. Discernment involves action. It also involves a decision. And the very first decision is whether it's about *my* life and *my* vocation or whether it's about *God's* will for my life and my vocation.

Back in the 1980s, a man named Robert Bellah coauthored a book called *Habits of the Heart*. In this book he talked about a crisis back in the eighties that he called "expressive individualism." Basically expressive individualism is the mind-set that I just described. It says that in order to be me, in order to be happy, in order to be completely fulfilled, I have to find the job, the relationship, the vocation, the career, the whatever that will completely capture me, and then I'll be able to express myself to the world.

That was back in the eighties, and now what do we see? We see young people who are trying to decide on their careers; they are trying to decide what they are called to do. What do they want to do with their lives? When it comes to their major, when it comes to their career, a lot of young people have the idea that "I should be able to just be myself and get paid for it." We see some of them on Instagram—they want to make a career out of just holding a camera and saying, "Blah blah blah blah blah." This self-expression is often a perfect example of the expressive individualism Robert Bellah wrote about. He says that we end up with a bunch of individuals who are looking out for the individual.

I don't know if Robert Bellah was Catholic, or even if he was Christian, but he goes on to say that the remedy for expressive individualism is *vocation*. The remedy for expressive individualism is the idea that my life is not just *my* life. Vocation means that we are called out of ourselves. We're living our life, and at some point, God steps in and says, "Okay, I'm calling you out of yourself. Calling you out of your life. I'm calling you to participate in my life. I'm calling you to look up from yourself and look at others."

When I was in seminary, one of my fellow seminarians was an older man who had a lot of maturity, a lot of experience. He had great observational skills, too. He said, "Here at the seminary, it seems like we're just a bunch of navel-gazers." He had a point; we were always saying, "What does God want? I don't know. How am I doing?" He said, "We're always looking at ourselves, always trying to figure out ourselves instead of looking up and saying, 'Okay, God, where do *you* want me to go?'"

You see, it's not "God, what do you want from me so I can be fulfilled?" It's not "God, where do you want me so I can express myself?" Instead it's "God, where do you want me to serve?"

A vocation is almost always oriented toward others. It's looking up from yourself and seeing where there is a need. That's why Robert Bellah was able to say, "The cure for expressive individualism is to look at the person next to you. What's their need?" Then it's looking inside yourself and saying, "What do I have that can serve this person's need?"

It becomes the opposite of self-fulfillment, the opposite of self-expression. It becomes self-donation. This is the first principle of discernment. It involves a radical reorientation of what we think our life, our discernment, our vocation means. Is it for me or is it for others?

TWO:
THREE LEVELS OF VOCATION

. . . .

EVERY VOCATION involves sacrifice. Some of my married siblings tell me, "Oh, Father Mike, we're so grateful for your sacrifice. We're so grateful for what you offer—so grateful for what you give." I look at them and say, "Yeah. I get to go to sleep when I want. And rarely do people wake me up in the middle of the night because I need to change them." I mean, it happens. But rarely. The point is, no matter what God calls us to, there will be sacrifices. I always say that the vocation of marriage and family is where bad people go to die. Marriage is the vocation where bad people go to die to themselves out of love for their spouse and their kids.

So when you're trying to discern what vocation God might be calling you to, coming at it by asking "Which one will fulfill me?" is the wrong approach. It comes down to this: Is my vision for my vocation for self-fulfillment and self-expression, or is it self-donation? Ultimately my life, my will, my purpose, all comes down to answering these questions: What is God's plan for my life? What is God's will for my heart? What is God's purpose for my life?

That's what your vocation is, and that's also what holiness is. St. Maximilian Kolbe explained holiness this way to the novices in his community. On a chalkboard he would write this equation:

w (your will) + W (God's will) = S (Sanctity)

Sanctity is when my will conforms to God's will. That's sanctity; that's holiness. That's it. That's the whole thing. Holiness is not a matter of not sleeping because you're praying all night. It's not a matter of fasting all day. It's never a matter of serving this way or that way or the other way. It's all about your will conforming to God's will. That's holiness. That's sanctity. That's what it is to be a saint. That's what your vocation is about. There's nothing less and nothing more than that.

In the Our Father, Jesus taught us to pray, "Thy kingdom, thy will be done." We pray that all of the time, but do we mean it? Do we live it? Because regardless of any vocation you might feel called to, ultimately you're called to holiness.

THREE LEVELS OF VOCATION

When it comes to vocation, there are three levels. The first is the universal call to holiness—your will conformed to God's will.

Every human being on the planet is called to be a saint. That's why Leon Bloy said, "The only real sadness, the only real failure, the only great tragedy in life, is not to become a saint."

There are a lot of tragedies in life. But the only real tragedy, the only truly devastating one, the only thing you cannot recover from, is to get to the end of your life and not be a saint. No matter how much suffering we go through, no matter how much loss we go through, the only real tragedy in life is not to have been a saint. The universal call to holiness is known as the primary vocation. The universal called holiness never changes.

The second level of vocation is what we typically think of when we think of *vocation*: the call to the priesthood, to married life, to consecrated single life, to religious life. That second sense of vocation might change once or twice in a person's life.

The third level of vocation is: What is God calling me to today? What task has he given me today? What is the season he's placed me in today? How is he calling me to say yes on a moment-by-moment, day-to-day basis? This sense of vocation changes a lot over the course of our lives.

The first sense of vocation never ever changes. This is your destiny. As Catholics, we believe in destiny. Destiny is not the same thing as fate, by the way. Fate is when you're fixed; you don't have a choice. Destiny simply implies *destination*.

God has created every human being in his image and likeness with a destination in mind, and that destination is him. It never changes, even if you make terrible decisions. No matter who you are or what you've done, you're called to be a saint. And I want to press pause on this for one second. Many of us have been raised in the Church; we've been raised Catholic. We've heard our whole lives that God loves us, but most of us do not really believe that. Most Catholics believe that God tolerates them. And so you might find yourself thinking, *God's called me to holiness, and he's kind of upset with me, and he kind of tolerates me, but I can't trust him. I can't trust Him, so I'm hiding from him.* If that's you, realize that his call for you, his love for you, has not changed. Even if you say, "I'm off the rails right now," you're called to be a saint, and nothing less than a saint.

The second level of vocation is what we typically think of: married life, priesthood, religious life, consecrated single life. But I look at this a little differently . . .

I was doing marriage prep for a couple, and about two weeks before the wedding, the bride said, "I don't know—I think I'm called to be a nun."

Okay, let's talk about that, shall we? I said, "Well, why do you think you're called to be a religious life?"

She said, "Well, I just want to live in poverty. I desire to serve the poor. I desire to live a very simple life. I desire to sacrifice myself."

I said, "Okay, so I know a lot of married people who live in poverty. I know a lot of parents who serve those in need on a daily basis. I know a lot of people who are in a family who have very simple lives. I think you can do these things and still be married."

Sometimes we reduce this second level of vocation by asking, "What are the jobs?" Someone might be considering the priesthood but think, *I don't know, I don't really like talking in public.* Someone else might think, *Should I be a nun? I don't know, I don't know if I like "nunning."* But that second level of vocation is really about asking, "What is the primary relationship by which I'll become the person that God wants me to become?"

If you're discerning marriage, the relationship with your spouse will be the primary relationship God will use to form you into the person he wants you to be. The relationship with your spouse is the way you'll die to yourself for Jesus and become the person he wants you to be.

As a priest, the primary relationship by which I'm meant to become the man God wants me to be is as the bridegroom to the Church, the bride. The primary relationship for me in this part of my life is with my students on campus; it's to die to myself for them. That's the primary relationship to which I'm called. God wants to make me holy that way.

For nuns and religious sisters, their primary relationship is as a bride to Jesus, the Bridegroom. These women become the women God wants them to be by being brides of Christ, the Bridegroom, and it's lived out in their relationship to those in their religious communities and to the people they serve outside of those communities.

For those called to the single life, their primary relationship is to their neighbors and their work colleagues. They are literally called to love their neighbor. My friend Ennie Hickman told me, "I think I have a sense that when Jesus commanded us to love our neighbors, he actually literally meant to *love your neighbor*." Your neighbor—the person who lives next door to you.

As a single, that primary way that I'm called to be a saint is by serving the people around me who have a need. Who are the people in my parish who have a need? Those are the people that I'm free to serve.

The point is when we are discerning our vocation, what we're really discerning is the primary relationship God is calling us to focus on. This kind of vocation might change once or twice in our lifetime.

And then there's the third level of vocation, where we discern the tasks we're meant to do. "God, what do you want me to do today?" This one is super exciting. And it's one of the reasons why we need to live—really live—in the Holy Spirit. For example, getting up today, I had no idea what God wanted me to do. I didn't know a thing. I didn't know if my plane was going to be on time. I didn't know if *I* was going to be on time. I didn't know what God wanted. My guess is that it's the same thing for you. You can show up for work, you can show up for life, you can show up for anything. And you've got your plan, but you pray, "God, I really want to be disposed to what you want. So what's your will for me today?" The answer to this question changes all the time. The first level of vocation never changes. The second level only changes once or twice. But this third level of vocation changes moment by moment.

So how do we figure out what God wants? Whenever you face a decision, you first can ask yourself a very dangerous question: "If I choose this, am I seeking to please the Lord, or am I seeking to satisfy myself?" Seeking to please God means you want to live for him; satisfying yourself means you care more about expressing your individuality. My guess is that a lot of us struggle with that second question.

The danger here is that a lot of us don't really believe that God loves us. We only think he tolerates us. And one of the dangers in that way of thinking is we conclude that God always wants us to do the hardest thing. Whatever thing I don't want to do, that must be what God wants me to do. This is a lot of people's default.

When they're tired, their default is thinking, *Would God want me to go to sleep right now? He probably wants me to pray.* At a restaurant they're getting ready to order and they think, *I can order the steak and potatoes, or I could order a kale salad. I bet God wants me to have the kale salad.*

The idea is that whatever is most difficult, whatever I least want to do, that's probably what God wants for me. At the heart of that is not God's will. At the heart of this is what I'm afraid of. This kind of thinking stems from the fact that I don't actually trust God.

But what if instead you were be able to say, "Would this please God? Would this please my Father's heart?" Not "Is this what the tyrant wants?" but "Would this please the Father's heart?" It's also recognizing that all those things you love please God. Think about it: Many of you are parents. And when your child chooses to do something that brings them joy, doesn't it bring you joy? Why would our heavenly Dad be any different? The things that bring you joy bring the Father joy too.

So the question is, "Am I seeking to please myself or am I seeking to please my Father?" Get back to this truth of who the Father is. In the very beginning when Adam and Eve, our first parents, turned away from God, they turned away from the Father. It wasn't that they stopped believing that he existed. But they stopped trusting that he was their dad. We see this in the way they listened to the serpent about eating from that one tree in the middle of the garden. God had told them not to eat the fruit of that tree so they wouldn't die. But instead of trusting him, they listened to the serpent. "You won't die! God knows that if you eat of this tree, you'll be like him. You'll have so much more life, and God doesn't want you to have that."

St. John Paul II says the first temptation is a temptation

against God's fatherhood. And ever since that moment that we have doubted God's fatherhood. "No, I don't believe he's my dad. He's a tyrant." What happened as a result of Adam and Eve's disobedience is that trust died in our hearts.

That's why when we approach God and say, "God, what do you want? What would please you?" we're afraid that he will demand of us the most difficult thing, the thing we want the least, the thing that's hardest. But what if the thing that brings us the most joy is what God wants? What if the very thing that will bring us the most freedom is what God wants?

When my will conforms to God's will, that's sanctity—that's holiness. That's the highest form of self-donation. It's way beyond self-expression.

Let's look at the story of Gideon. God calls Gideon, the least person of the least tribe of Israel, to fight. God speaks to Gideon. He says clearly and directly, "Gideon, go lead my people into battle."

Gideon isn't ready to trust, so he says, "How am I supposed to know that's you speaking, God? I'm not sure, so here's what I'm going to do. I'm going to take some fleece and put it out in the yard, and in the morning, if the fleece is wet but the ground is dry, then I'll know it's you."

The next morning, the fleece is wet, and the ground is dry. Gideon still isn't sure. "Okay," he says to God. "It's a good start. I don't know if I can really trust you, though, so I don't know if that's a clear enough sign. I'm going to put the fleece out again, and in the morning if the fleece is dry but the ground is wet, then I'll for sure know it's you."

And God does it.

I hear this story and think, "What the?" I'm praying every day, saying, "God, come on. Just give me a little hint. Give me a sign. Give me something." And I actually know people who had a similar story to Gideon's.

Fr. Kevin, a priest I know, tells a story of when he was just out of college. He had gotten a job teaching, and at one point he was on a retreat, praying with a bunch of monks in a monastery. They were all chanting the evening prayer, and suddenly it sounded as though someone had taken the volume and slowly turned it down.

He looked up, and now he couldn't hear anything. He could see everyone's mouth still moving. *That's weird*, he thought.

And then he clearly heard this voice: "Kevin. Why are you fighting me?"

He responded, "What?"

"Kevin. Why are you fighting me?"

And he knew what the voice was talking about. And then, very slowly, the volume was turned back up to normal.

Afterward he was talking to one of the monks. "Hey, here's what happened to me," he said, and then described it. "Is that normal?"

And the monk said, "No. No, that's . . . that's unique. You should listen to that."

I was in college when Fr. Kevin shared that story with me, and I thought, *Yeah! God, do that!*

Because I wanted the clear sign. I wanted the clear voice. *Just point me in the right direction, God, and I'll go.*

But God knows so much better than me, obviously, and maybe he knows better than you too. You see, I started praying when I was fifteen or sixteen years old, "God, if you want me to be a priest, just let me know." All through high school and college, I prayed that prayer. I'd add, "I don't want to do it, but if you let me know, I'll do it—I'll become a priest."

God is so good because he did not let me know prematurely. And when he did reveal it, I remember thinking, *God, if you would have revealed this even two weeks ago, I wouldn't have been ready.*

I think I would have still said yes. But it would have felt like taking a square peg and trying to fit it into a round hole by pounding on it with a hammer. "Okay, fine, God! Okay. I'll do it. Whatever."

But God is so good. He waited an extra ten years, and then I was able to say yes with freedom and joy.

THREE:
DECISIONS AND DISCERNMENT

. . . .

WE MIGHT SAY, "Oh, I just want God to let me know what he wants; I just want to do his will," but truthfully that's often false. If we're honest, what we actually want is relief from the anxiety that comes along with the responsibility of making a big decision.

A lot of times, I don't really want to do God's will—I just don't want to be nervous anymore. I don't really want to know God's will—I just want to know. Then I'll be done with it. And not only that—I want to know what God wants so I don't have to make a decision.

Not wanting to make a decision is one of the key reasons we have to step back and realize something about discernment: God always speaks in clarity.

I used to have this image that discernment was all about signs. I thought God was a little like Sherlock Holmes. People have no idea what's going on, and then Sherlock Holmes would say, "Oh, that little piece of hair on the chair reveals such and such." We do this a lot of times with St. Thérèse too. Someone does a novena to St. Thérèse, and at the end of it, they add, "God, if you want me to do this thing, give me a rose." Don't get me wrong—I like Saint Thérèse. I'm not bashing her and her flower stuff. I like it.

But sometimes on the last day of the novena, a person thinks, *Okay, where's the rose? Where's the flower?* Someone else might say, "Well, I didn't really see a flower, but I met a girl named Lily, and she had red hair so it's kind of like a rose." We're always looking for the mysterious sign. But God speaks in clarity.

Or someone falls asleep and has a dream. They wake up and say, "In the dream I was a nun," or, " I'm married to such-and-such person. What does it mean?"

It probably means you had beef stroganoff for supper. It might not mean anything. Because God speaks in clarity. If I wake up from that dream and I don't know what God wants me to do, then it probably was just a little indigestion. Or maybe it was on your brain.

But let's say you come out of a dream and you know exactly what to do. You are convinced. "Wow, this is very, very clear." That's the time to take a step. Because God always speaks in clarity. Always.

Often he speaks in ways that are not very romantic. They're not exciting. They're not super-dramatic. He often speaks through one of the Ten Commandments. "I'm really discerning this relationship with someone who's married. God, what do you want? . . . I can't tell. So I'll just pursue this and see where it goes. And God, if you want to stop me, go ahead and stop me."

God already has revealed his will on these kinds of things—through the commandments. Through the Church, guided by the Holy Spirit. Through Scripture.

God leads us through the Holy Spirit as well. Of course, we have to trust that the Holy Spirit is actually active and alive in us. Otherwise, it's just a nice idea. We have to trust that not only are we guided by the Church and by Scripture, we're also guided by the Holy Spirit. And we're guided by our past. We're guided by our experience.

Back when I was discerning priesthood, I always wanted to know the future. "I want to know the future, God. Just let me know the future. If I walk down this road, where will it go?" or "If I leave this job and take that job, what will happen?"

I was talking to a young man yesterday who's becoming a carpenter. He's apprenticed to a master carpenter. But he's consumed with questions. "Should I go into ministry? Should I go to seminary? If I work for this guy, he actually wants me to take over the business. He wants me to own the company. I could buy him out in six, seven years from now. Here I am, nineteen years old, and I can own my own company in seven years. What should I do?"

I told him he should just take the next step. We can't know the grand plan, but we can know the next step. That doesn't mean that we'll know the second step or the third step after that. None of us can know the future. It's one of the reasons why Jesus tells us not to have any anxiety about the future. It's futile, because we can't ever know it.

So you can't know the future, but what can you know? You can know your past and you can know your present and you can know what you're called to. You've lived your life. You know how you act. You know how you live. You know what you've done. You know your past. You know where you are right now. And you also have a vision of what God wants for you. Not whether you should enter the priesthood, religious life, or married life. The vision you know God wants for you is this: he wants you to be a saint. You can look back at your life and say, "Is there a trajectory that God has me on right now?" And then you can take the next step, trusting that it will all work out. And it will.

I was a missionary after college for a year in Belize, right on the border of Guatemala. That's when the Lord won me back to his Church, and to his heart, and it was awesome. But then the questions started: "Should I be a priest or not?" (I was getting ready to marry this gal, and I thought I should figure that out beforehand.) I had a renewed fervor for "I need to know."

During my time in Belize, I received a letter from a priest I knew in college, and he said, "Mike, listen, you can never know the future, but you know your past. You know the ways that God has spoken to you in the past. You know where he's led you in the past. You know where you are. So what's the trajectory?"

The same thing is true with your life. You know your life. Where has God been leading you? When he spoke to you, where did he lead you? When you said no to him, where did that lead you? You'll be able to say, "Okay, that's my trajectory."

A week later I got a letter from another priest. He said something like, "Mike, this is your life." It helped me realize, "Oh my gosh, Lord, you have been leading me to this place." We can never know the future, but we all know our past. We all know where we are now, and every single one of us knows one thing for certain: God wants us to be a saint.

So where is he leading you? He's leading you into the future, but none of us can know it. That's called wisdom. Wisdom is knowing my past, knowing where I am, and knowing God wants me ultimately to be a saint. And this is important: God wants you to be a saint more than he wants you to be a priest. Or to be a nun. Or to be married. He wants you to be a saint more than he wants you to be any of those things. That's why this is a secondary vocation. Your primary vocation is to be a saint. Knowing that, where is God leading you right now? What will lead you closer to that? *That's* what we discern. That's why we get to make decisions.

But often when it comes down to it, I still want God to tell me.

Why? Because then I'll have relief from anxiety. Then I won't be wrong. I don't want to choose the wrong thing or make the wrong decision. And here's something else: if God leads me this way, and it's hard or difficult and I don't like it, then I get to blame him. I can say, "God, I'm only here because you told me to be here." I don't want to be wrong. If it's not my decision, then I get to blame God, and that way I can avoid responsibility. However, God gives us the dignity of making decisions. God extends to us the dignity of taking responsibility for saying yes to him. For listening to his voice.

When I was in high school, I was trying to discern whether or not I should go to seminary for college. I visited a couple of seminaries, but I had no idea if going to undergrad seminary was the right decision. So I went to my dad for advice. He told me that when he was in college, he also wondered whether or not he had a vocation to the priesthood. He was talking with some priests, and he asked them if they thought God wanted him to be a priest. One priest he told him that if God was calling him to be a priest, he would always be called. My dad said, "You know, Mike, if you don't know right now, you're free to attend normal college if you want."

That highlighted something important for me. I had been thinking that if I said no to seminary and decided to go to a regular college instead, I would be saying no to God. But God never expects us to answer a question he has not yet asked. So while I was asking him, "Should I go to seminary or not? I don't know if you're asking me to do this, God," he was in effect saying, "Yeah, go ahead and choose."

Because God never expects us to answer a question he has not yet asked. He always speaks with clarity, and so if he hasn't yet asked something, then basically he's saying, "You have freedom. You have the freedom to make your own decision at this moment." Some of us might not like it, but that's how it goes.

TWO TRUTHS

In the next chapter, I'll go over how we make decisions. I'll share three questions that you should ask yourself each and every day. But before we get to those three questions, we need to know two truths.

Truth # 1: God loves you better than you love yourself. Every one of us knows that. We've at least heard it. Whether we believe it or not is another question, but God loves you better than you love yourself.

Truth #2: God knows you better than you know yourself. Think about those truths combined. If God both loves you better than you love yourself and knows you better than you know yourself, then what God knows you're made for is what he wants for you. What He knows will make you the most happy, that's what God wants that for you. What He knows will fit you best, that's what he wants for you.

We each have our own way of learning. God knows how you learn things, and so he'll teach you in a way you can understand—he'll communicate in such a way that you won't miss his voice. These two truths add up to one profound truth: you can trust him. You can trust Him. You can begin your day—and live your day—with this knowledge. "Oh, God, you love me better than I love myself, and you know me better than I know myself. I can trust you!"

Once you know that you can trust God, really trust him, you're ready to ask him three questions.

FOUR:
THREE QUESTIONS

I RECOMMEND three practical questions you can ask God. If you aren't sure that God loves you better than you love yourself or that he knows you better than you know yourself, then you don't really trust him yet, and these questions are intimidating. But once you know you can trust him fully, you'll be ready to ask these three questions.

QUESTION #1: AM I IN A STATE OF GRACE?

This first question is really practical. It's not "Do I feel like I'm in a state of grace?" but "Am I in a state of grace? Am I conscious of mortal sin?" Now, on the campus where I work, there are students who go to confession once a week or once every two weeks. We have confession every day, which is awesome. But a lot of times when I'm working with youth ministers or DREs, they tell me, "Yeah, it's been a couple years, Father." The neighboring parish is a little bit far away, or whatever. There are lots of excuses.

So even if you're involved in ministry at your parish or at your college, it might still have been a while since your last confession. The big question, if you want to be able to discern God's will for your life, is this: Are you in a state of grace or are you conscious of mortal sin?

If you're not in a state of grace, recognize that being connected to God and having open communication with him means that God can always reach us, even if we're in the middle of mortal sin. Even when we're in the middle of mortal sin, we can go to confession because God has something called *prevenient grace*. This means he can reach out and grab us and bring us back. Whenever we go to confession, it's really God moving first. It's not us going to confession and saying, "Hey God, I know you might have forgotten who I was." No, he brought you there. When you need him the most, he wants you the most. Let me say that again: When you need him the most, he wants you the most.

And if you're not in a state of grace? Trust him and go to confession.

QUESTION #2: AM I PERFORMING MY DAILY DUTIES?

Are you doing the tasks you have for today? Why is that so important? Because God's will is in your daily duties. If you cannot find God's will in this moment, you will never be able to find God's will, because God's will is only in this moment. He doesn't have a will for your past. He only has a will for right now. God is only present to you in this moment. God is present in all moments, but He's only present to you in *this* moment.

You can look at your schedule and say, "Okay, Lord," as you get up at whatever time you need to. "Lord, I'm getting up as a yes to you. As I go to work, Lord, I go to work as a yes to you. As I have that meeting at work today, I'll go to that meeting as a yes to you. As I call that person, I'll make that call as a yes to you." When you see all the tasks on your calendar, see them as God's will for your day. That means that every single day, at every moment, you get to say yes to him.

Every time you do whatever you're supposed to do, you're saying yes to him. What happens is that you practice saying yes to God on a regular basis. Then, when God reveals his big "Here's my call for you," you'll be able to say yes just like you do it all the time. That big yes is really not a big yes—it's just another yes. Are you doing your daily tasks? Are you saying yes to God when you say yes to your calendar? If you are, that big yes will be easy.

QUESTION #3: DID I PRAY TODAY?

Here's why this is important. Years ago I attended a conference led by Father Larry Richards. Everything was behind schedule, and instead of being able to speak for an hour as planned, he only had five minutes.

He condensed what he had planned to say and told the group, "Here is what you need to know." He said that if you are doing ministry in the Church, if you are working with youth in the parish and you are not making a daily holy hour, then you need to get out of ministry. Now you might think sixty minutes is out of the question, but could you manage to spend twenty minutes with Our Lord on a daily basis? (I'm nicer than Fr. Larry—he's a tough guy). But can you commit to spending twenty minutes with Jesus every day?

This time with Jesus is not because you need something. This twenty minutes is where you just get to know him. It's being in his presence and letting him love you; it's getting close to the Father's heart. Twenty minutes is possible, isn't it? That's not even a Netflix episode. I tell my college students that if they're having trouble finding twenty minutes a day to pray, they should start an episode of Netflix—that's their timer. I tell them to put it on mute, and when the episode is over, they're done praying.

Netflix is just like eating Doritos. You know how it goes. You start out thinking, *This is really tasty,* and then you forget to stop. Suddenly you think, *Oh, now I feel sick*. How many times has the same kind of thing happened when it comes to streaming television shows? You think, *Oh, this a really good episode*. And then you watch twenty more. Those of you who are married and have kids are like, "Never! This has never happened to me." And those of you who are single are like, "Yeah, all the time—last night in fact."

Archbishop Harry Flynn was the archbishop in St. Paul–Minneapolis, when I was in seminary there. The week or two before we got ordained, he invited all the guys getting ordained over to his place. We had a holy hour with him. After the holy hour, before he had supper with us, he got up and said, "Men, I need you to do this. If you are going to be priests, this is important. You need to make a daily holy hour. Here's why: you're going to get involved in ministry. You're going to be talking to a lot of people, doing a lot of things. And there will be things you say that you shouldn't have said. There will be things you do that you shouldn't have done. There will be things you should have said that you didn't say and things you should have done but you didn't do. Making time for a daily holy hour means that you get to come in front of Jesus and allow him to remind you of things you should have done or said; you're letting him have your heart. Otherwise you'll just be plowing through your ministry, not even giving him a chance to correct your course."

When you don't take the time to pray, suddenly you realize that you're just going through the motions. You'll start to feel like you're serving God the CEO of God, Inc., rather than working with your *dad*. At some level you'll begin to think, *I'm working for God, Inc.—the pay's crappy and the benefits are awful. I don't know why I'm here. No one respects me.*

But when you see yourself as working with your dad, you think, *Wow, I get to work with my dad on a daily basis.* With that perspective, you can keep serving, pouring your lives out for people who might not seem to pay attention. They might not seem like they care, but you continue to give. But now you realize that you're not doing that alone. You're working with Dad. That's really powerful.

It's really important to remember that you're not just working for the Church; you're pouring yourself out with Jesus. As you lay down your life, you're laying down your life with him. And you need strength to do that. That's why you let him have your heart on a daily basis for twenty minutes. And it's not twenty minutes to pray using a prayer card or praying a rosary—you don't have time for that in this twenty-minute segment. This is not the time to read the Bible. You just have time to do one thing, and that's to let him love you.

If you make it a habit to ask these three questions, I can absolutely guarantee you will never, ever, ever miss your vocation. You'll never ever miss God's call for your life. The channels will be open and connected to him. You'll say yes on a regular basis. And by giving him at least twenty minutes every day, you'll be giving him time to say, "Hey knucklehead, wake up—here's what you need to do." You will never, ever miss out on discerning God's will for your life.

FIVE:
THE DOOR

. . . .

WHENEVER YOU HAVE to make a decision, it's similar to facing a door.

Should you walk through the door? What decision should you make? There's really a practical way to figure that out: you can ask yourself four questions:

1. Is this door a good door? (Is this decision a good decision?)
2. Is this an open door?
3. Is this a wise door?
4. Is this a door I want to walk through?

So first you must determine if this door is a good door. Is this decision a good decision? If it's an evil thing to do, it's not God's will for you. He doesn't want you to do that. So if it's evil, then, move along. Is it good? Great. Is it neutral? Wonderful. That's an option then.

43

Now it's time for the second question. *Is this an open door?* Is this even a door that's actually available to me? For instance, I might think it would be good to play in the NBA. And I think God's calling me to do that so I knock on that door—and they say, "Get out of here, punk. You're not NBA material." Okay, that's a closed door to me in my life . . . I'm getting over it.

The point is, it's a closed door. You know, sometimes people forget about this part of discernment. You can discern that something is a good door and you really think everything is pointing in that direction, but when you go up to the door, it's closed because of someone else.

A man came to me for spiritual direction, and he told me that he had fallen in love with this woman and was praying about marriage. He was in a state of grace, he was praying daily, and he felt like she was the one. So he proposed to her, and she said yes. On our first marriage prep session, they were sitting together on the couch, and I began explaining what was going to happen, what was involved. Suddenly she looked at him and said, "Um, we need to talk. I think I'm going to leave." And she broke up with him just like that.

He said, "Wait a second—I did all the right things. The three steps. I discerned. This seemed like it was what God was calling me to do. Why did this happen?"

I said, "Well, I don't know, but just keep moving forward, dude. The right one is out there." He begins dating another girl, a year passes, and they break up. He dates another girl, and months into it, he's still praying, still in a state of grace—the whole thing. He finally proposes and she says yes.

Two months later this girl breaks up with him. Different girl, same scenario. He asks me again, "What's wrong? I thought I was discerning this."

And it was hard for me to say this, but I said, "This *is* discernment. You discerned yes. The first one discerned no. And now so did this one. So is this a good door? It's a good door. Both women are great gals. Is this an open door? No. It seems like a great door, but it's not an open door."

This happens a lot with people discerning a vocation to a particular religious community. They might feel God wants them to join the Dominicans, the Franciscans, or some other order. They feel certain of it. They fill out an application. Now it's time for the community to discern. The applicant discerned yes, but the community discerned that the door was closed. That's part of discernment. That's discernment working. It can be painful. But that's discernment actually working out.

"Is this a good door?" Great. "Is this an open door?" If yes, that's awesome. Then it's time for the third question: "Is this a wise door?" Would it be wise for you to make this decision? This is when you go back to the idea of knowing yourself, knowing your past, knowing who you are. And knowing the person you think God is calling you to be. Would this decision please the Lord? Would this be wise? Would this help get you to that place where you think you know God is calling you to go?

Here are two quick things, if you're at question number three, to keep in mind for yourself today.

The first one I've already mentioned: discernment requires action. A lot of times, we think, "Okay, here's the data that I know right now. Pondering this won't get me too far. I won't know what next step to take, so what I need to do is I need to get more data." So take action. Who do you need to talk to? Do you need to visit a seminary? Do you need to visit a convent? Do you need to get off your butt, walk across the room, and ask that girl on a date? Because until you take action, you won't know more data, and until you know more data, you won't know what to do.

The second thing to keep in mind is this: you can only discern one vocation at a time. What do I mean? I get emails roughly five times a week from someone (either it's the guy or it's the girl) who says something like this: "I'm dating this person who's seriously considering a religious vocation. What do I need to do?" "He says he's breaking up with me because . . ." or "He says he can't date me because he's discerning this, but he wants to keep me kind of on the side, kind of a back pocket, safety net kind of a thing."

Okay, pause. I understand this is heart stuff, and it's sensitive, and I want to be very careful, but the reality is we can only discern one vocation at a time. What that means is I can't simultaneously be dating someone and discerning religious life. I can't be dating someone and discerning the priesthood. I can discern this relationship. If you're dating someone, you discern that relationship. I can't be in the seminary and also discerning, "Well, maybe I should date that cute librarian at the seminary library." I can't be in the convent and saying, "You know that boy from back in high school? Maybe I should discern whether I should leave and date him." You can only discern one vocation at a time. So if you're in a relationship, discern that relationship. Is this what God is calling you to? Should you pursue this or not? If you're in the seminary right now, don't be discerning a potential romantic relationship. Discern the seminary. If you're in the religious life, don't spend time thinking, "Maybe God's calling me to some other thing." Discern this particular vocation. Discern where you are. You can only discern one vocation at a time.

As you can see, answering the four questions gets progressively more difficult. Discerning whether a door is a good door or not is usually pretty obvious. Is this an open door? Again, this is usually relatively obvious. Is this a wise door? Okay, I've got to use my brain now. And often this is one of those times you just want God to tell you. But if you are in that place, you are going to hate the fourth question. Because the fourth question is: "Is this a door I want to walk through? Is this a door I want?"

There's something really good about this last question, because it's God saying, "I want to have a relationship with you. I'm not just going to boss you around. I'm not going to tell you that you have to go here or go there. I want you to walk with me. Do you want this?"

Here's the thing: if God has not revealed that this is his call specifically for you, then you have a decision to make. It's as though he's saying, "Yeah, if you want to, you can go ahead. If you don't want to, it's okay too." Because in reality, if you walk through any of those doors, guess who's going to be on the other side?

God is going to be there. Even if you make a terrible decision, one that not only was not good, but was evil. You can call out to God; he's going to be there. Even if you chose a locked door, God's going to find you. It was not a wise decision, but you barged through it. Now you've come to your senses—this is the story of the Prodigal Son. He made a stupid decision, an evil decision. His father let him do it. And then, when he decided to come back home, his father was there.

Sometimes we're too afraid of making a wrong decision. We think if we make a wrong decision, we won't be the best. We won't be maximally fulfilled. Or maybe it will wreck everything. It's rare that a decision wrecks everything, but it happens. Remember, though, that first sense of vocation can't be wrecked. At any moment, we can come to our senses and say, "God, what am I doing? I'm going to go home." At any moment, no matter what door we walk through, at some point we can say, "Wait a second, in my Father's house there are slaves who are better off than I am. What am I doing? I can go home."

The only real tragedy is getting to door number four and not saying yes.

SIX:
QUESTIONS AND ANSWERS

Q. WHAT DOES HOLINESS REALLY MEAN?

A. We have an idea about the saints that they were super boring, and they dressed weird. They lived unlike the rest of us. And they were perfect. I heard a story about Mother Teresa, how she could really lean into people; she could really be kind of cranky. Sometimes she was really hard; like the rest of us, she wasn't gentle all the time.

My favorite saint is St. Jerome. He's the one who translated the Bible. He could also be called the saint of sarcasm—he is the saint of jerks basically. He could be super caustic and abrasive—which, by the way, are two words that the seminary used to describe me. I'm very grateful for someone like St. Jerome because he wasn't perfect. St. Catherine of Siena is another awesome saint, a doctor of the Church, a phenomenal woman.

Recently a young woman told me she had just read a book

claiming that St. Catherine of Siena had an eating disorder. She fasted a lot, but the reason she fasted a lot was because she had an eating disorder. She lived off the Eucharist, but the author of this book said she did that because she had an eating disorder. And then she died early, because her eating disorder led to her premature death. The young woman and her friends were very disturbed about the idea that St. Catherine of Siena might have had an eating disorder.

So I asked my spiritual director about it. He is an eighty-four-year-old hermit who lives in a secluded cabin in the Northwoods. Visiting him is a little like visiting Gandalf. I said to him, "Father, I don't know what to do here—all these girls are freaking out—what if St. Catherine of Siena had an eating disorder?" (Now, it's very likely that she didn't. It's a relatively new phenomenon apparently.)

My spiritual director said, "And?"

"Well, what if the reason she did all this penance was that she had self-loathing?"

"So?"

"What if it led to an early death? What if she died early because of this?"

"And?"

"What do you mean?" I asked him.

"So, even if that was the case, which it probably isn't, it just means that God sanctified her with her wounds. God sanctified her in the midst of her wounds."

This is the case with all the saints. Whatever they struggled with, whatever they wrestled with in real life, God sanctified them. It doesn't mean that he made them perfect, or that they were awesome to be around all the time. It just means that in the midst of their wounds, God was able to make them holy.

And what is holiness? It's not long vigils; it's not fasting all the time. It's not living at the church. Holiness is not working in the Church, either.

Holiness is my will joined to the Father's will; this equals sanctity. And you don't have to know your vocation perfectly either. Lots of people say, "I can't wait to find my vocation because then God can really make me a saint."

No, if God can't make you a saint right now, getting married is not the answer; becoming a priest or a nun is not going to change that. You're already on your way. Right now is when God wants to make you a saint. He's not waiting for you to say vows; he's not waiting for you to make a promise; he's not waiting for your circumstances to change. He wants you today—just today—to say yes to him in your daily duties.

If you were to say, "I've discerned that I'm not going to work in the Church anymore; I'm going to go work for Microsoft instead," God can sanctify you through that. He can sanctify you maybe even more through that than through what you're doing now. The reality is that God can sanctify you anywhere. It's a really good question, though, because we think we have to be somewhere else in order for God to make us holy.

Q. WHY DOES IT SEEM THAT SO MANY OF THE COMMANDMENTS ARE "DON'TS"?

A. This is a common perception for many of us. In fact, G. K. Chesterton pointed this out. He said that it makes sense that God would point out the don'ts, the things we shouldn't do. He went on to say there are so many things we *can* do—if God started saying, "Here's all the stuff you *can* do," it would be unending list. The shorter list is, "Hey, just don't do that." Think about all the trees in the garden; there was just one God told Adam and Eve they couldn't eat from. (That's why I always say that with Adam and Eve, it was the original, "You had one job. You tanked it.")

Think about this world. Think about this life. When I think about God's goodness, I remember that Jesus said we should call God *Abba*, meaning "Daddy." I'm not comfortable calling God "Daddy," though, so for the last couple months I've just been calling him "Dad." Every time I do it, it always hits me: "*This* is what Jesus meant." It's that closeness of a dad. I love my earthly dad. And I love being able to talk to "*the* Dad."

Our Dad has put us in such an abundant world. "You want to do that? Go ahead and do it." "This will bring you joy? Go ahead and do it." Right now I'm looking at the mountains surrounding L.A.—they are incredible. On the other side there is the ocean, and that's incredible too. People are hiking and surfing—it's all amazing. God said, "Yes, go enjoy it!" Go home, and love the people you live with the best you can. If you like programming computers, go do it. There's no rule that says you can't. There are so many times God says, "Just go do it!" along with that smaller times he says, "Hey, don't do that."

Q. HOW DO YOU PRAY FOR AND HELP SOMEONE ELSE DISCERN? YOU DON'T REALLY KNOW IF THEY'RE IN A STATE OF GRACE, OR PRAYING DAILY, OR FULFILLING THEIR DAILY DUTIES. HOW DO YOU HELP THEM?

A. That's a great question. You can simply say, "If you want to know God's will, just ask yourself these three questions." Share the three questions, and then let the Holy Spirit move them.

Q. IS BEING SINGLE AN ACTUAL VOCATION?

A. Not everyone will agree with this, but I think when there is a call to the single life—if there is a call to the single life—I think it's a call to make a decision, rather than just a default. Now, whether that decision is actually a public consecration, or a private decision where a person says, "Okay, God, here's where I am with my circumstances. I'm making the decision to enter into this singleness as a gift."

St. John Paul II pointed to the fact that the single life, whether it is a temporary thing or whether it's for the rest of your life, you are called to use this singlehood to serve. To make a self-gift.

I wonder if one of the main reasons John Paul had this idea

was that one of the most significant people in his life was a man named Jan Tyranowski. Jan Tyranowski was a tailor in Poland. He never married; he was single his entire life. There was no sign that he was consecrated in any way. But the local parish priest said, "Hey, Jan, you're single. You're available to serve, so can you start this rosary group here in Varitsa?" He agreed, and he got some youth together to pray the rosary. Young John Paul was part of this group.

Jan Tyranowski was captivated by John of the Cross and was very knowledgeable about him. At first, John Paul said he did not like Jan Tyranowski at all. It's like that today. You might go to a youth group and be put off by the leader, but later on you change your mind and think they're awesome. That was John Paul's experience with Jan Tyranowski. At first he was put off by how hardcore Jan Tyranowski was.

Later on John Paul was completely won over, and Jan Tyranowski so impacted John Paul II concerning Carmelite spirituality that John Paul wrote his dissertation on the spirituality of St. John of the Cross. In the end, Jan Tyranowski might have been one of the most significant people who shaped John Paul II's life. And it was all because he used being single to make a decision to serve the people around him in his parish.

How to Make Great Decisions is based on a talk
Fr. Mike Schmitz gave at the Los Angeles Religious
Education Congress in 2017. He currently runs the
Newman Center at the University of Minnesota–Duluth
and is also the director of youth and young adult ministry
for the diocese. Schmitz's engaging messages on his YouTube
channel have attracted over one million views, and he
continues to inspire people in their faith all over the globe.